Patterson, Geoffrey.
The story of wool / Geoffrey Patterson. -- London : Deutsch, 1987.
32 p. : ill. ; 19 cm.

03070050 ISBN:0233979239 :

1. Wool trade and industry -- History. I. Title

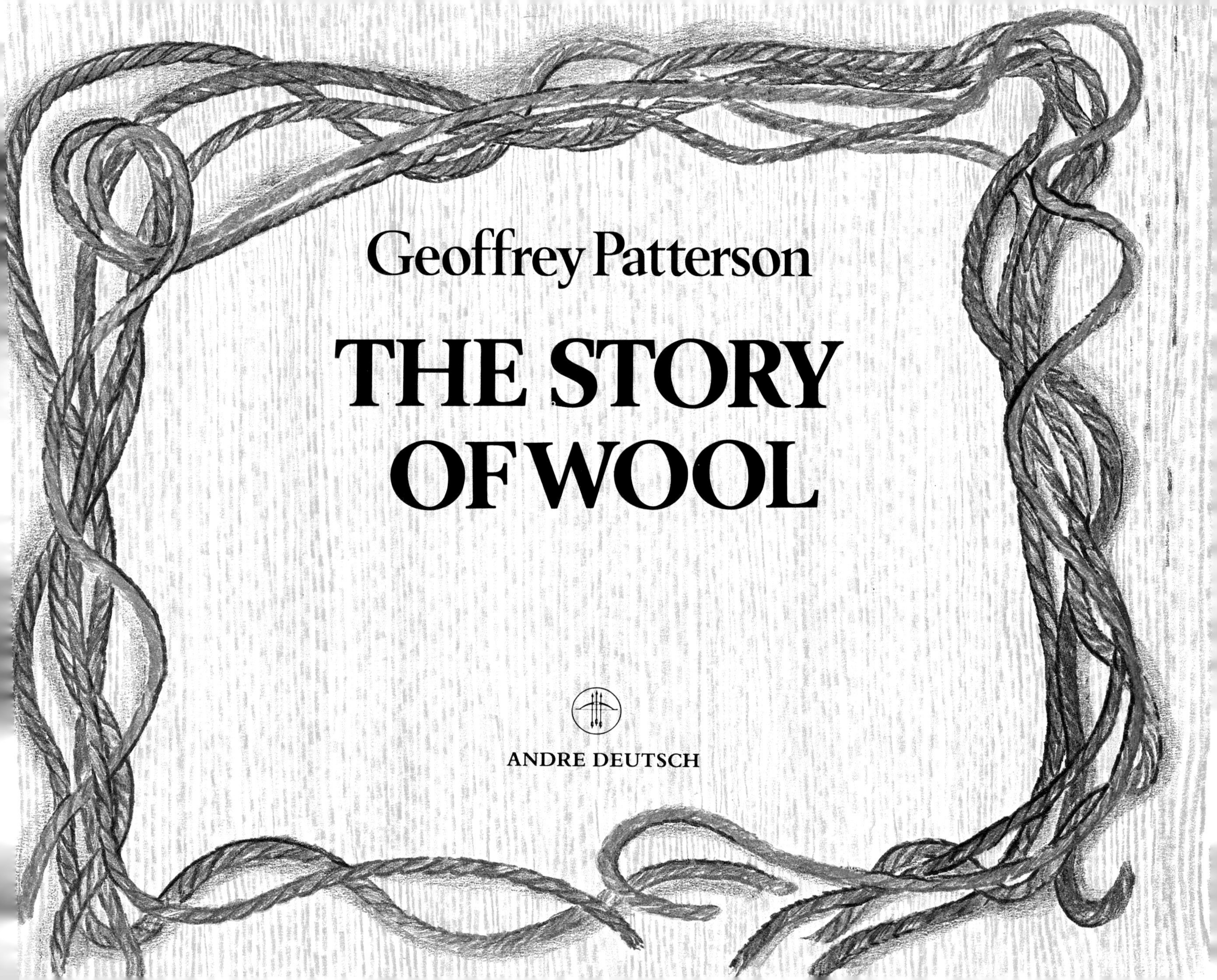

Geoffrey Patterson

THE STORY OF WOOL

ANDRE DEUTSCH

Acknowledgement

The British Wool Marketing Board
Oak Mills, Station Rd, Clayton,
Bradford, West Yorkshire BD14 6JD

Dedication

FOR RUTH AND OLIVER

First published in 1987 by
André Deutsch Limited
105–106 Great Russell Street, London WC1B 3LJ

Printed in Belgium by
Henri Proost, Turnhout,

ISBN 0 233 97923 9

INTRODUCTION

Wool from the sheep's back has been keeping people warm for thousands of years, and remains a favourite material in spite of competition from synthetic fabrics. Its natural fibres are stretchy and resilient, so clothes made from wool are comfortable and keep their shape. It is light as well as warm and it will take a downpour rather than a shower to soak you if you're wearing wool.

Records show that wool was bought and sold in Babylon as long ago as 4000 BC. Babylon, incidentally, means 'land of wool'.

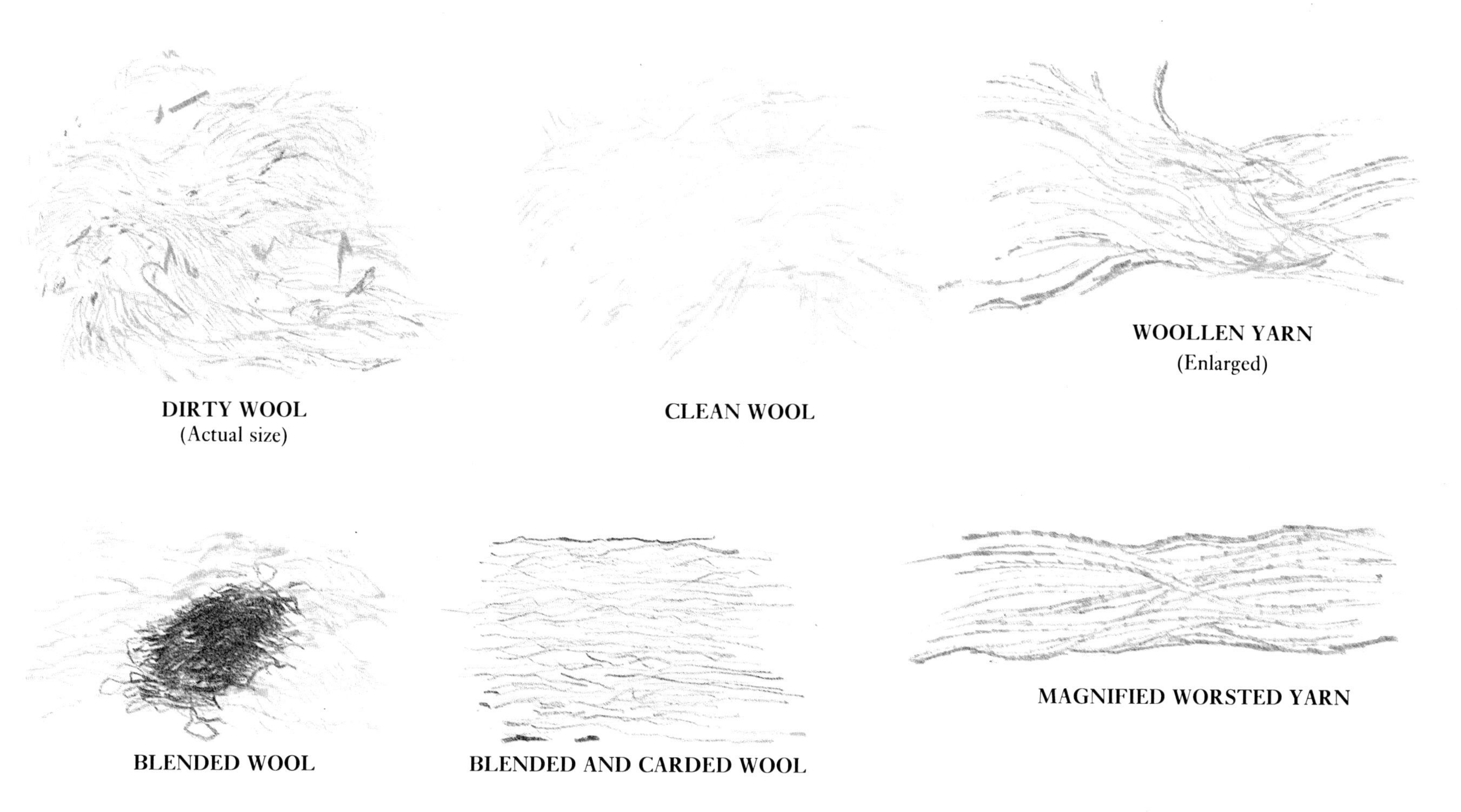

The long process of turning wool into clothes – or rugs, blankets, chair covers and carpets – begins on the farm with the sheep the farmer decides to rear. The different breeds produce a great variety of fleeces, some of which will make fine, smooth yarn, others which are more suitable for spinning into chunkier, thicker thread.

Before wool can be spun it must be washed thoroughly to remove grease and dirt, then blended to achieve the right texture. At this stage the process changes according to the kind of yarn the manufacturer wants, woollen or worsted. Worsted yarn, which makes an even, smooth fabric is spun from long combed or carded threads of similar length. Woollen yarn is spun from fibres of variable length which are intermingled to produce a bulky yarn with a surface that feels fuzzy to touch. All worsted yarns are woven into cloth; woollen yarn is either woven or spun in a continuous thread for knitting wool.

The many breeds of sheep in the world today come mainly from the Corsican Mouflon sheep (known in Neolithic times), the Soay and a long-woolled sheep bred by the Romans.
The very earliest farmers realised the value of sheep for wool and meat, and over the centuries the quality of both has been improved by skilled cross-breeding. The Border Leicester, for example, a favourite breed with a long lustrous fleece, owes much to work done by Robert Bakewell in the eighteenth century.

WENSLEYDALE LONG WOOL

SUFFOLK

HERDWICK

LEICESTER LONGWOOL

BLACKFACE

WELSH MOUNTAIN

There are as many different kinds of fleece as there are breeds of sheep. Some fleeces produce hard-weaving wool favoured by carpet manufacturers, others make a fine smooth yarn just right for dress materials or fine quality suits, yet others a long thread for knitting. One breed, the Exmoor Horn, has a fleece so soft and smooth that it is used for the finest cloth, in particular green baize for snooker and billiard tables.

STONE AGE

In the Stone Age, about 400,000 years ago, wild sheep were hunted for food. Stone Age people had no tools for shearing the fleece from a living sheep's back, nor did they know how to spin or weave, so whole skins were roughly stitched together to make clothes.

NEOLITHIC

Between 9,000 and 7,000 BC people began to herd sheep in flocks and to make cloth from their wool by cutting the fleece from the live animal with sharp flints, then spinning it into yarn for either knitting or weaving into cloth.

THE MOUFLON

CHEVIOT

Mouflon sheep, similar to those first hunted by Stone Age man, can still be found in Mediterranean countries in small flocks owned by peasant farmers. They are quite different from the highly bred Cheviot found mainly on the Scottish Borders. It is over 600 years since the forerunners of the Cheviot breed crossed the border into Scotland from the North of England. Today, greatly changed by skilful breeding, it produces almost one-fifth of Scotland's wool and is prized for its meat and its fleece.

Cheviot tweeds, with their distinctive colourings, have been famous for over 200 years and are still in great demand today.

The improvement of the fleece has taken place gradually as has the development of the huge, complicated machines which turn out millions of yards of cloth and knitting wool every year. Just as the modern sheep could not exist without his ancestors, so today's machines work on the same principle as those used by Neolithic men and women.

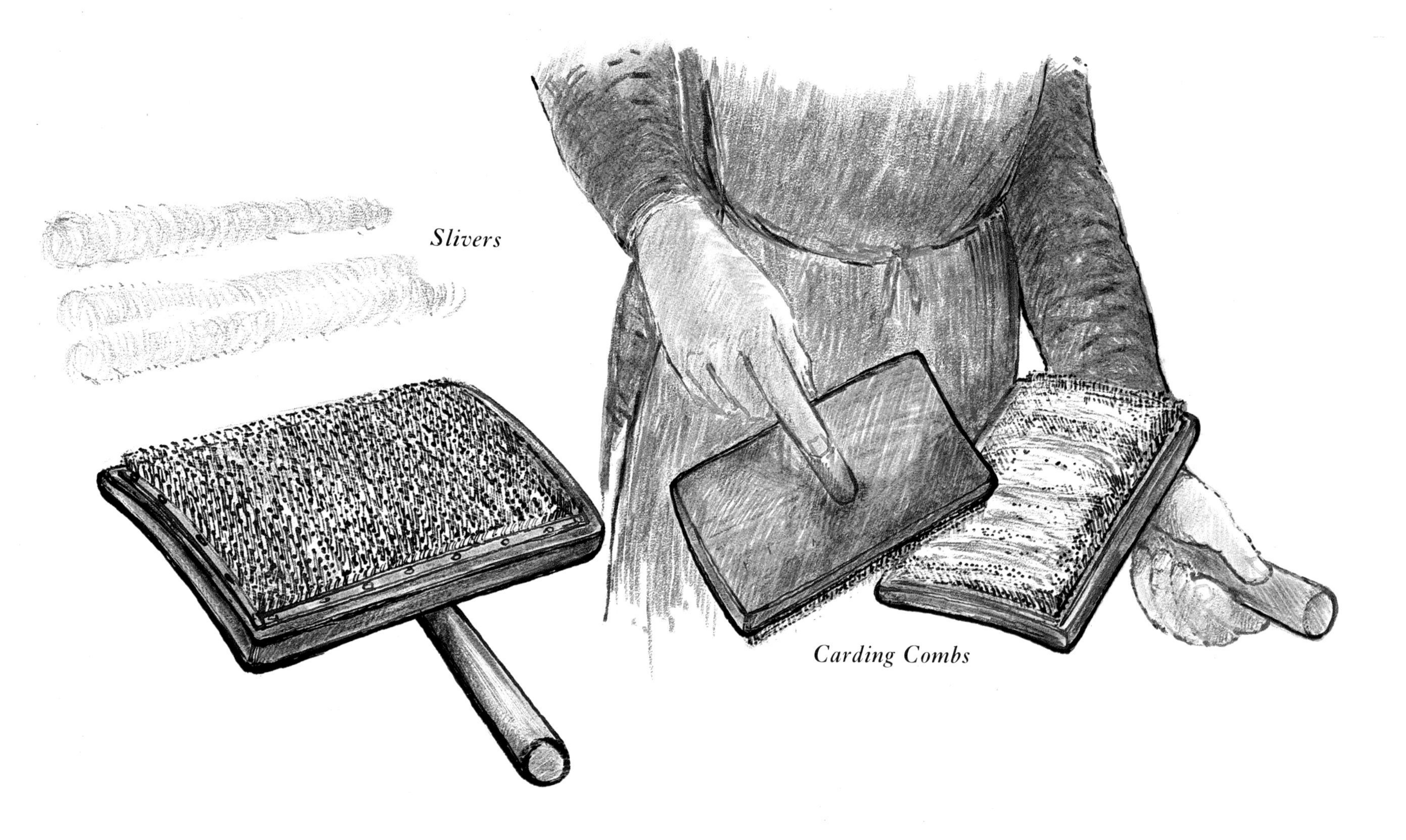

Before the raw wool can be spun it has to be combed or 'carded' to get rid of knots and tangles and form single fine strands. In factories this is done on huge machines, among the largest used in the textile industry. When the job was done by hand special brushes covered with bristles were used. A knot of matted wool was placed on one brush or 'card' and then brushed with the other until all the wool fibres had been separated and pulled into soft, rope-like threads called slivers. The springy wool slivers were then spun into yarn. There are still craft weavers and spinners working today who are able to comb wool by hand.

Drawing from Roman Vase

Spinning using Distaff and Spindle

The earliest yarn, coarse and uneven, was made by simply pulling out wool held in one hand with the fingers of the other and twisting it into thread.

Later, better yarn was made with a distaff, or short stick, held in the spinner's belt. Combed wool was placed on its top and then pulled out and twisted. The twisted yarn was fixed to a 'spindle', another stick, kept turning to twist the yarn tighter. The spun wool was wound onto the spindle.

Small round weights called 'whorls', made of stone, clay, lead or bone, were fixed to the bottom of the spindle to keep the weight on the yarn constant, and thus the thickness of the thread more even. The expression 'give it a whirl', meaning 'give it a go' comes from the word 'whorl'.

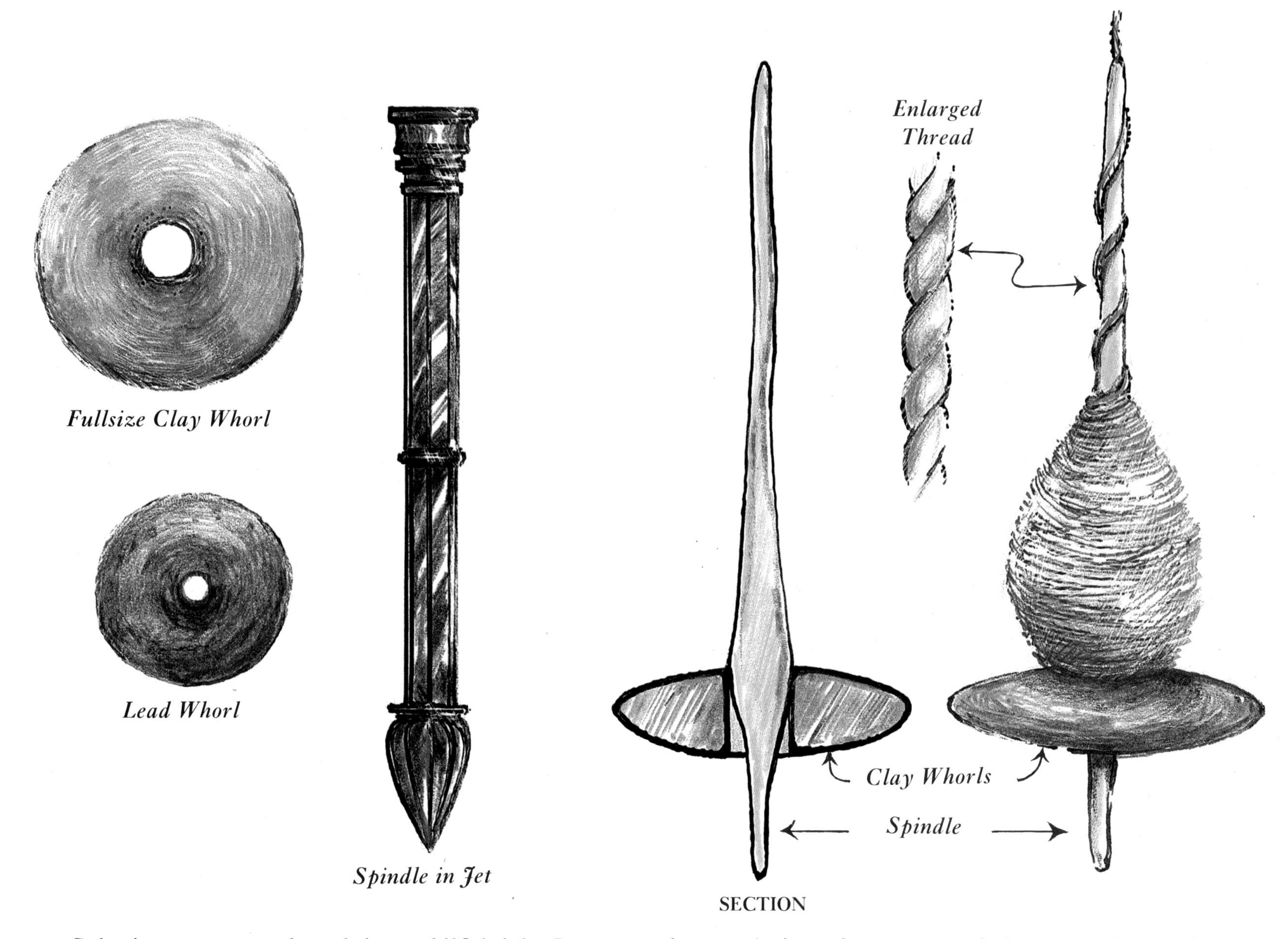

Spinning an even thread is a skilful job. It was traditionally done by women, and a woman who was a bad spinner was expected to make a bad wife; hence the term 'spinster' – an unmarried woman whose only task was to spin. For the same reason the female side of the family is still known as the 'distaff' side.

The spinning wheel was invented sometime between AD 500 and AD 1000. The spindle was mounted across a wooden frame and connected to the wheel by a pulley. One turn of the wheel sent the spindle spinning almost twenty times.

The earliest weaving looms were recorded about 2000 BC. Evenly spaced threads were threaded up and down in vertical frames. These threads, weighted with clay to keep them taut, were called the warp.

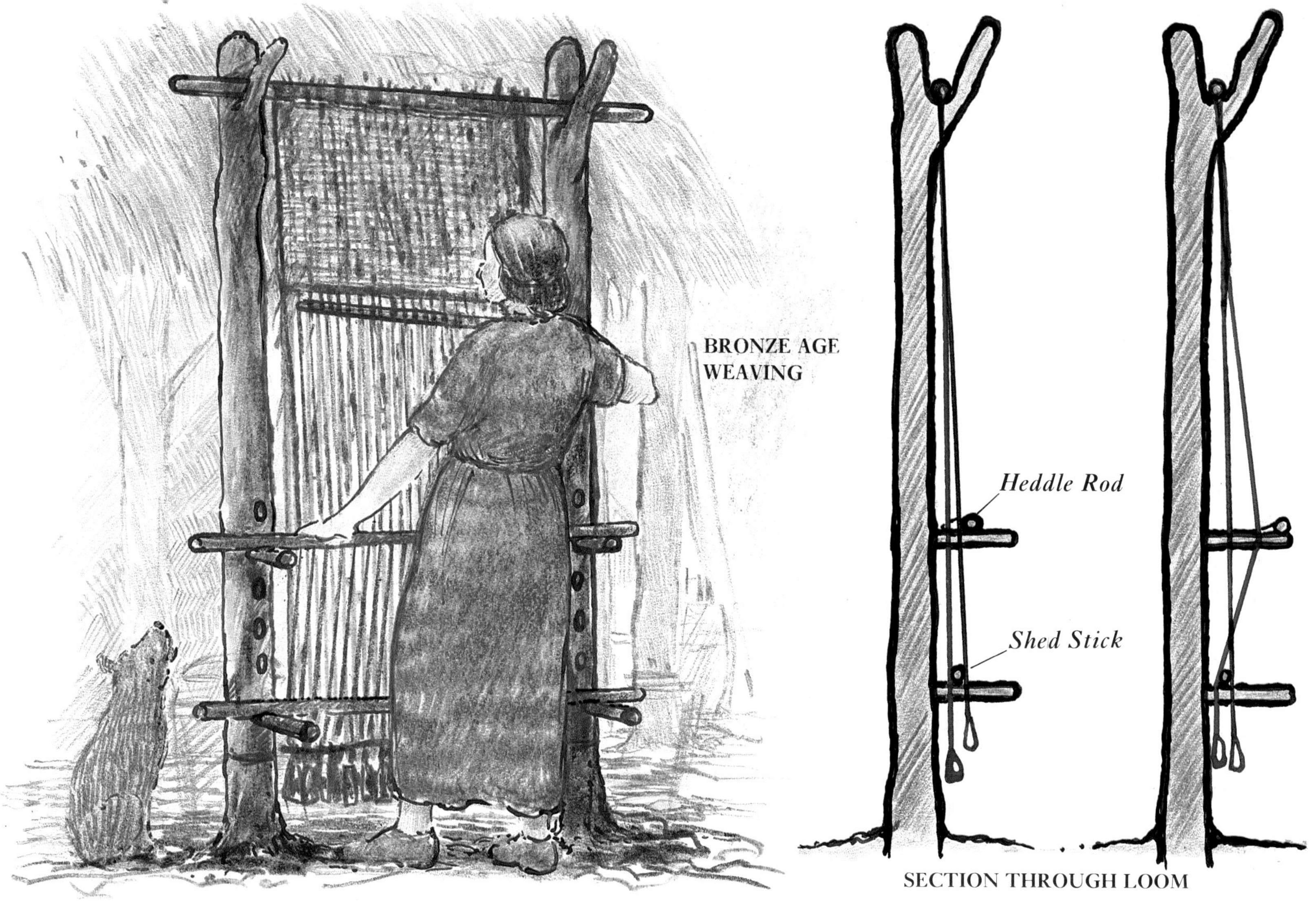

Alternate warp threads were then fixed by a loop to a stick called a heddle rod, which rested across the loom. The front and back sets of warp threads were kept apart by the shed stick.

Yarn, wound onto a shuttle and known as the weft, was then passed backwards and forwards through the gap.

Between each threading of the shuttle the heddle rod was shifted, bringing the back threads to the front. Today's great factory looms still work on the same principle, and so do you if you do something as simple as darning a pair of socks.

KNITTING

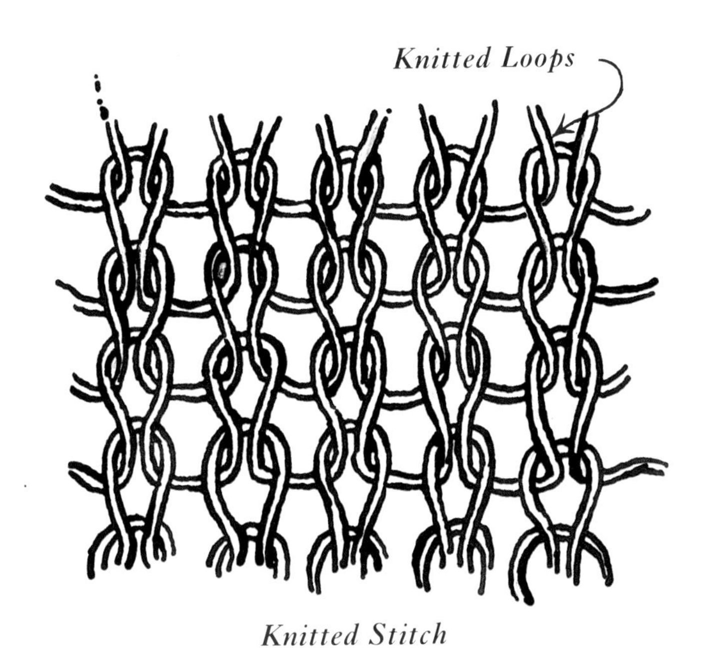

Knitted Stitch

WEAVING

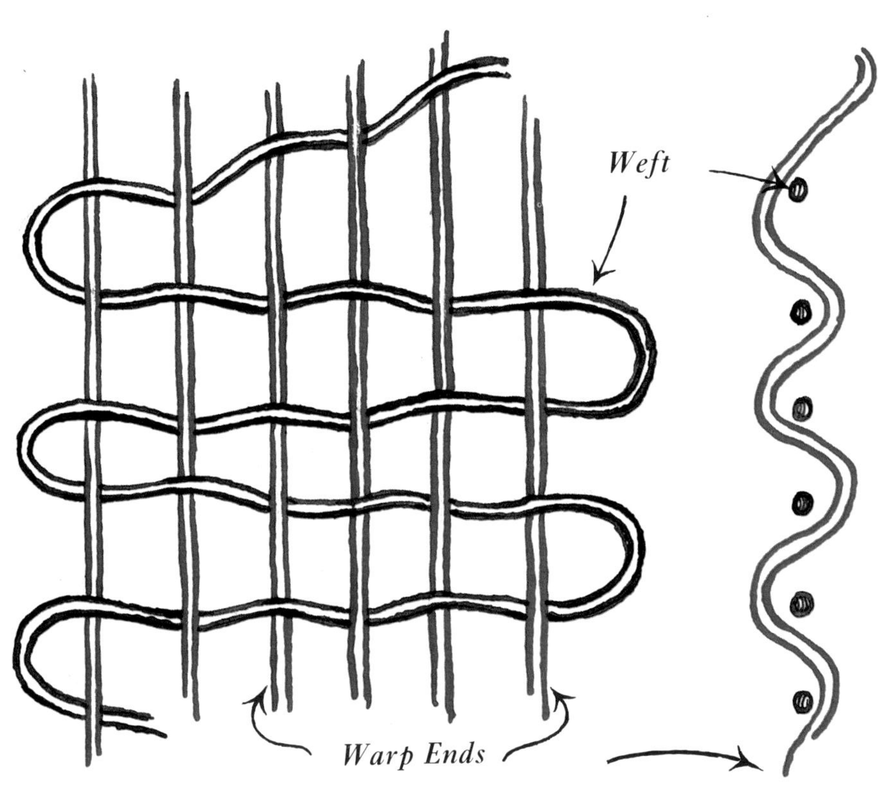

Woollen yarn is either woven into cloth on a loom or knitted. Knitted fabric, whether knitted by hand or machine, is made from rows of interlinked looped stitches. Knitting is an ancient skill; records of people weaving knitted garments have been found in Egyptian tombs dating back as far as the fifth century BC. Woven cloth is denser and firmer than knitted, the weft threads being pushed tightly up against each other as they are woven between the warp threads. Woven cloth is hard-wearing and, if the right wool is used, a woollen carpet, for example, can be trodden on for years before wearing through. In the same way, a good tweed jacket, woven from fine but hard-wearing yarn, can last a lifetime.

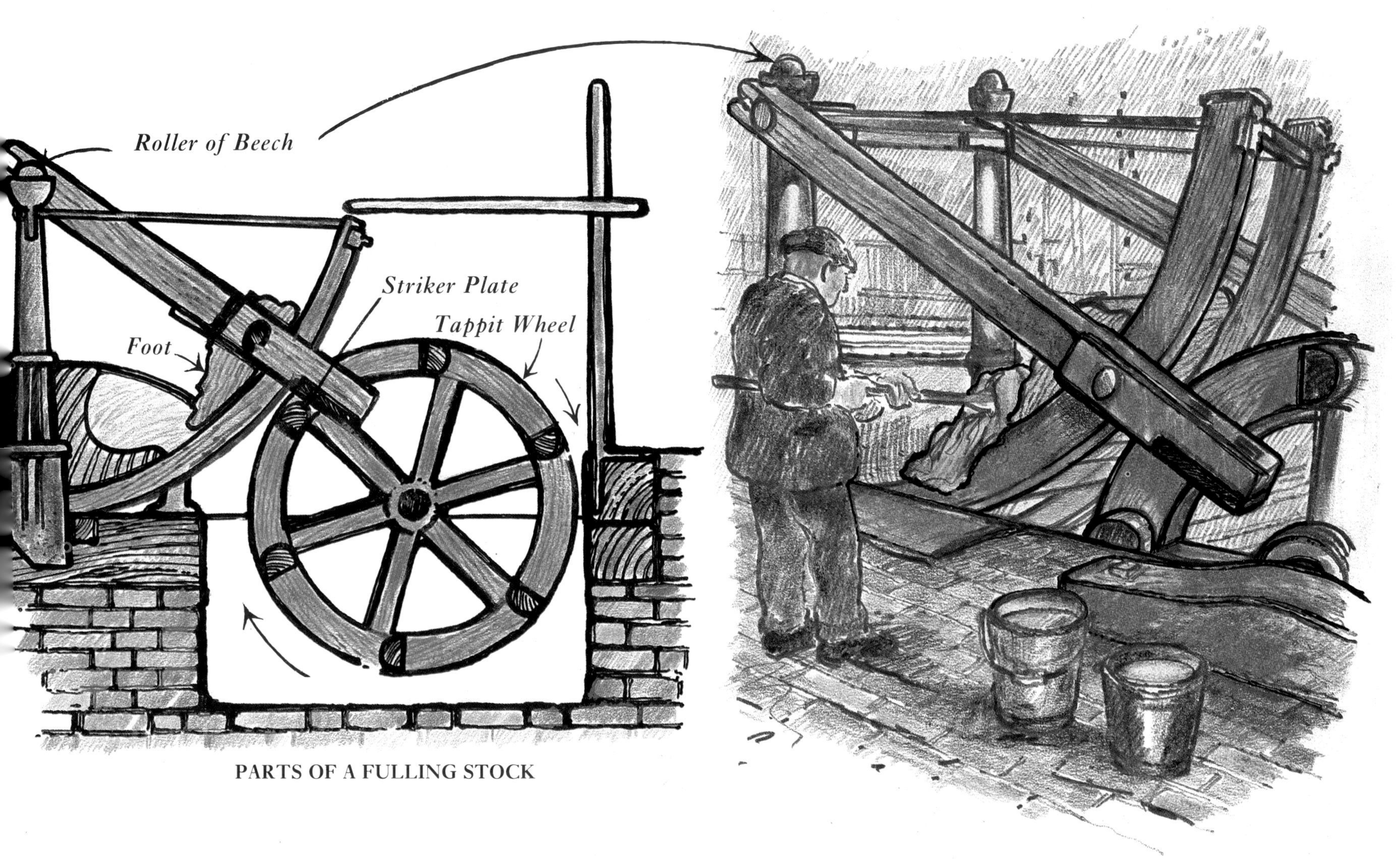

PARTS OF A FULLING STOCK

As soon as it was woven the cloth was washed thoroughly with Fuller's Earth to get rid of any remaining oil and dirt, to shrink it slightly and to flatten and soften the weave. At first this job was done by pounding vigorously with the hands and feet, but later water-powered mills were built near beds of Fuller's Earth.

The wet cloth was then fastened by hooks to frames called 'tenters', so that it stretched and dried evenly. This is where the expression 'to be on tenterhooks', to be on edge, comes from.

The man in the picture is feeding the cloth into the machine where it is pounded by the 'foot'. Between 60lbs and 120lbs of cloth were put in at a time.

During the fourteenth and fifteenth centuries there was a great demand for cloth, both in Britain and abroad, so towns connected with the wool trade grew in size and prosperity.

In Yorkshire and on the upland moors sheep produced heavy fleeces and there were plenty of fast running rivers to turn mill wheels. The great lords of the northern counties and the bishops established huge flocks at places like Jervaulx, Rievaulx and Fountains Abbey.

In the Cotswolds there was good grazing ground and a plentiful supply of the lime-free water essential for the washing and fulling of wool and cloth. Cirencester, Bradford-on-Avon and Stroud were busy centres for this area.

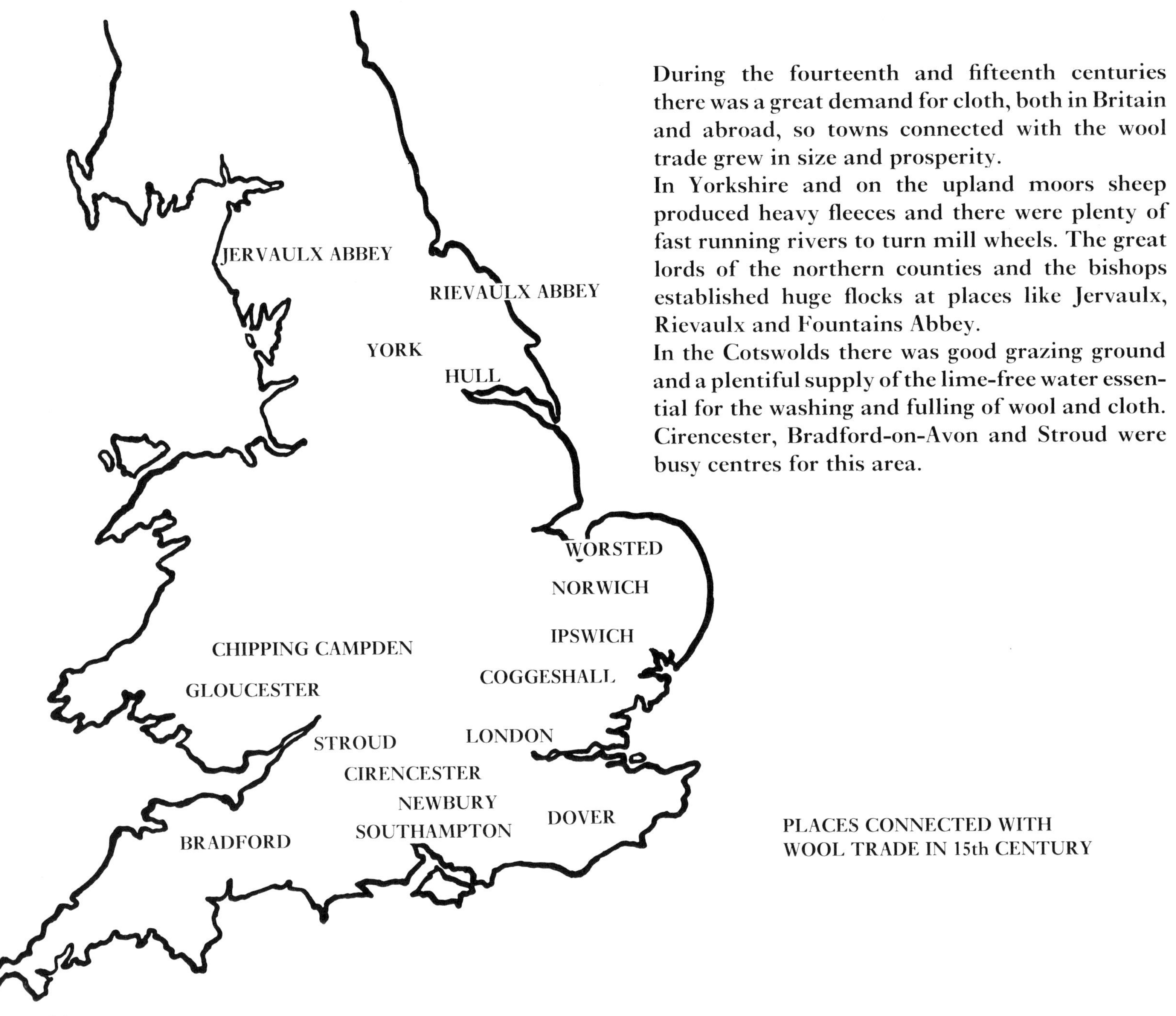

PLACES CONNECTED WITH
WOOL TRADE IN 15th CENTURY

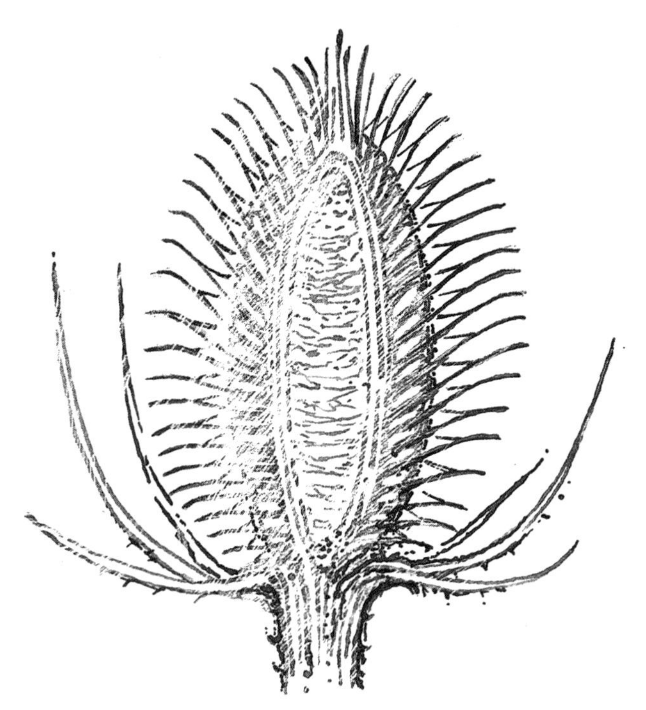

SECTION THROUGH TEASLE

From a stained glass window showing a monk cropping woollen cloth

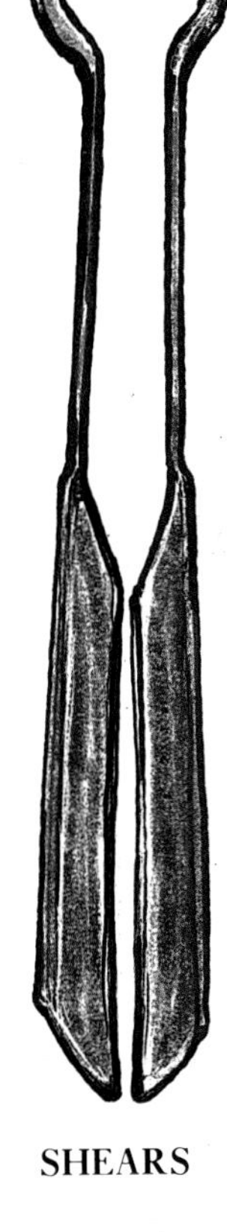

SHEARS

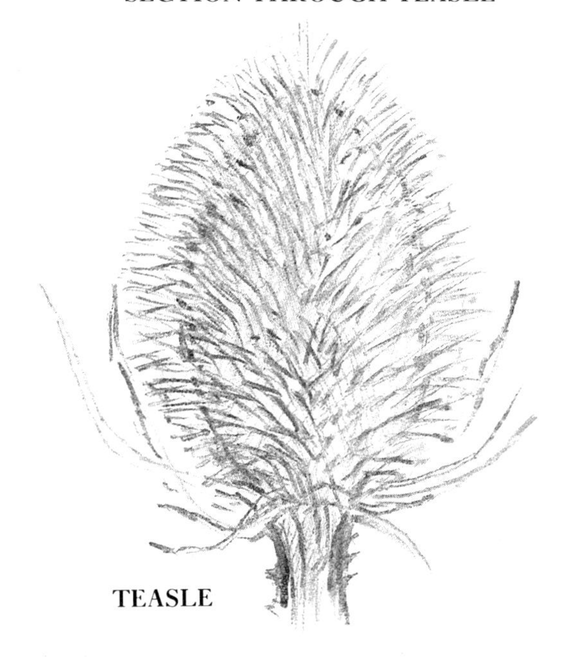

TEASLE

Cloth was brushed with teasles to give it a soft, fluffy feeling, then cropped with shears to smooth the surface. This was skilful work, as the shearer had to achieve an even surface without nicking the cloth.

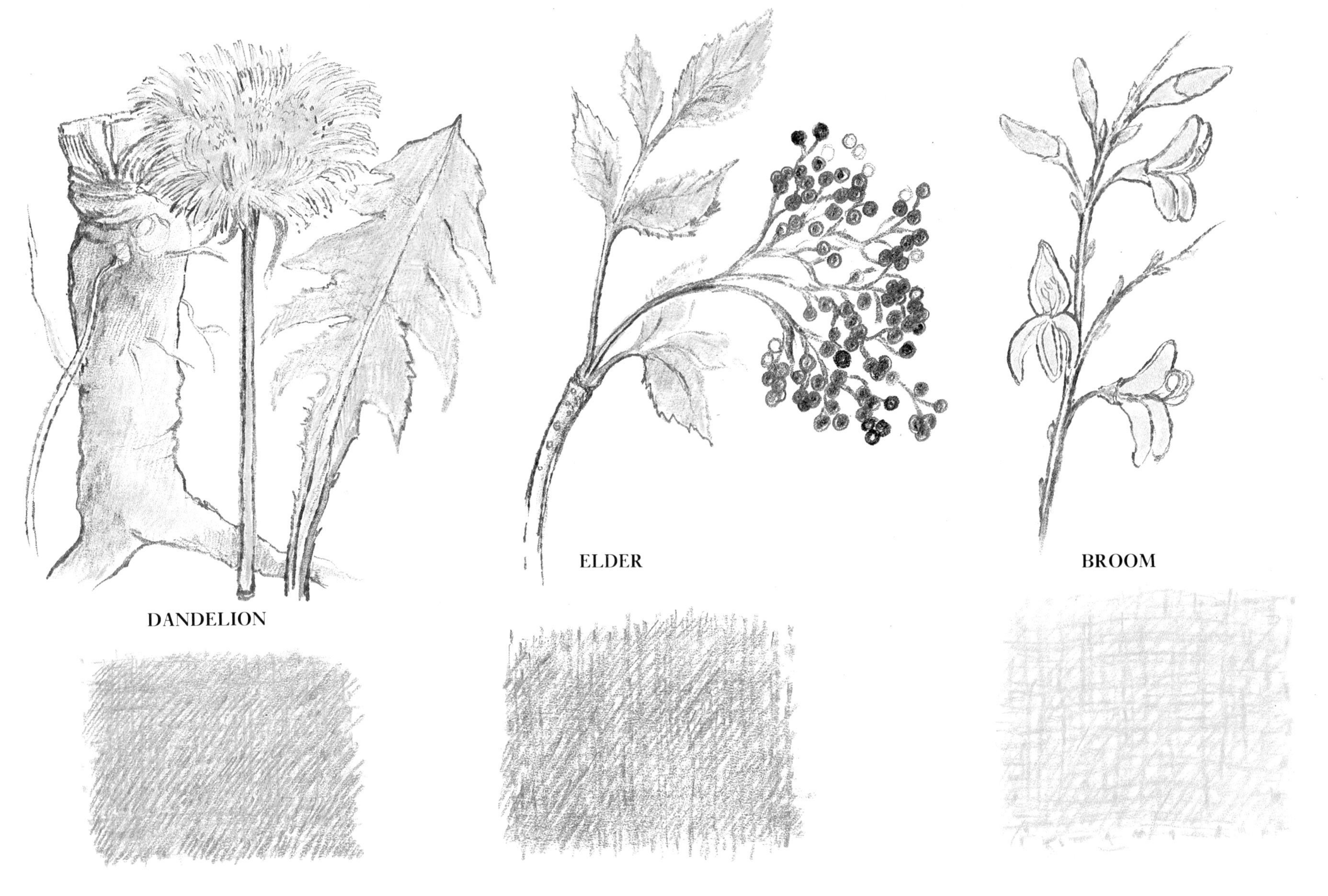

For thousands of years people have used plants and lichens to dye wool and cloth. They have also tried out 'mordants', substances which fix colours so they won't wash out. Wood ash, for example, fixes most colours, alum is particularly effective with scarlet, and as late as the last century dyers were still using the ammonia from horse urine to hold colours fast.

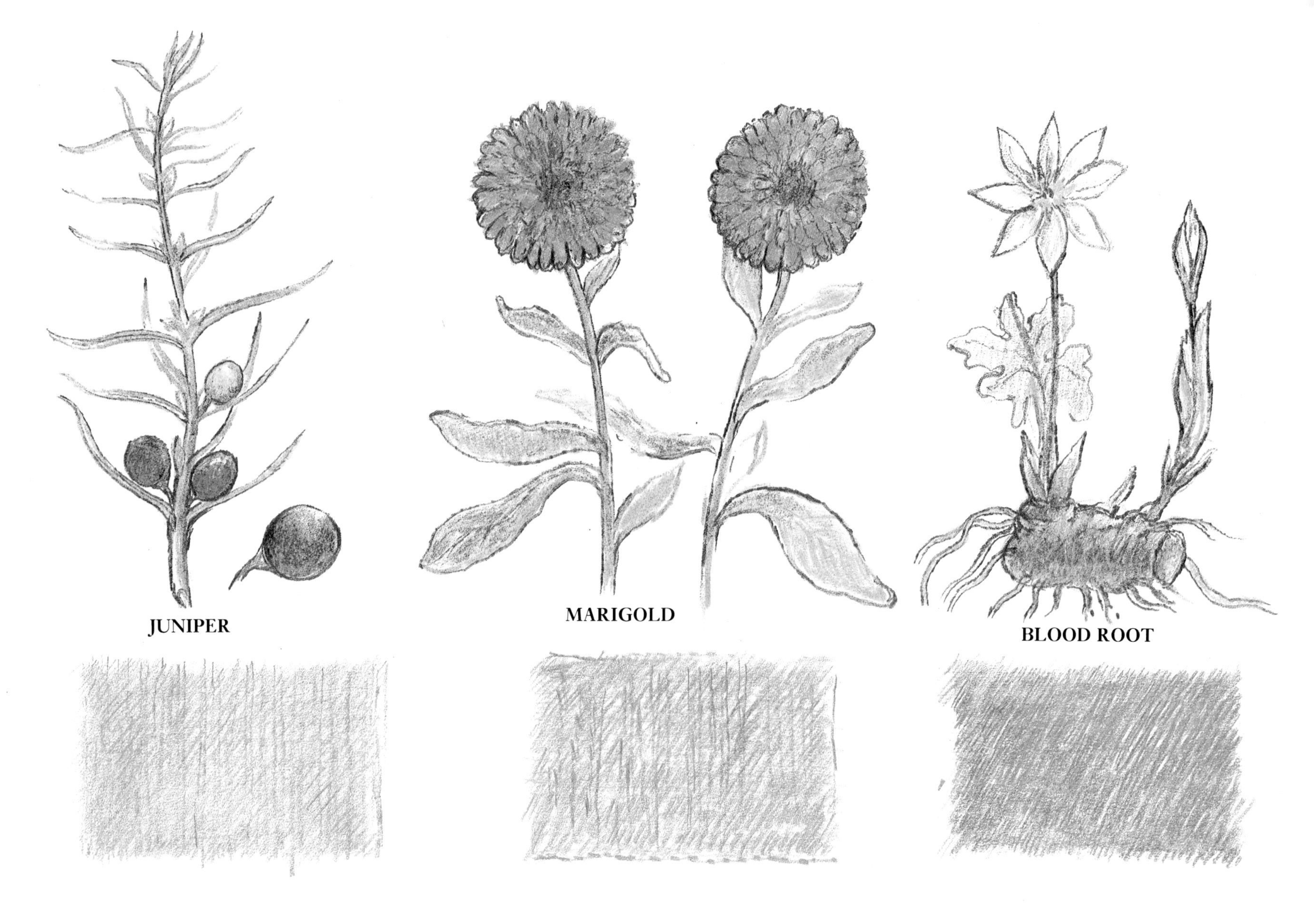

Natural dyes are beautiful, but it is hard to keep the shade the same for different batches of cloth. Today commercial colours are made from chemicals that can be measured exactly, so there is less variation in colour from one batch to another.

THE DEVELOPMENT OF THE WOOL TRADE

In medieval Britain there were sheep everywhere. The life of the poorest villager was made easier if he had a sheep or two to give him wool, meat and tallow for his candles, while landowners and high-ranking churchmen had huge flocks – one Bishop of Winchester is said to have owned 2,900.

The sheep was the country's most valuable product and important export. Merchants made fortunes out of wool and often spent their money on building magnificent churches – reminding us when we visit tiny villages how prosperous and busy they must have been.

Because wool was so important, wool workers became powerful enough to form themselves into Guilds. Weavers, Fullers, Shearmen, Dyers all produced cloth made to an agreed standard. Young men who wanted to become craftsmen had to serve an apprenticeship for five to seven years – worthwhile because the Guilds protected the interests of their members and looked after them when they were ill.

The numbers of sheep increased steadily and by the time of the Industrial Revolution (1750–1850) there were some nineteen million. Today the world's sheep population is up to about nine hundred and forty six million.

THE WOOLSACK

The Woolsack in the House of Lords at Westminster is the official seat of the Lord Chancellor. It symbolises the importance of wool to the country.

PACKHORSE BRIDGE AND WEAVERS' COTTAGES

Before factories were built, weavers worked in their own cottages. Light came in through rows of deep windows and there was usually a long room on the upper floor where the cloth was stretched.

When the cottages were by a river, bridges were built low and narrow to make it easy for pack horses carrying bundles of wool to cross.

SHEEP DIPPING

"A sheep's worst enemy is another sheep" they say, because disease spreads rapidly in a flock. Sheep are dipped against maggot-fly and other pests three or four times a year. 'Dipping' is compulsory and done in specially built 'dips', but till this century a stream was usually blocked for the job. It was worth the trouble because a washed fleece fetched more money.

SHEPHERD'S HUT

For a good deal of the year sheep graze freely in the fields and on hillsides, watched over by the shepherd and his faithful, skilful dog. He tends the ewes during lambing, cares for sick and injured animals and rounds them up at times like dipping and shearing.

In the past the shepherd often lived in a hut which was pulled to the field, or hillside, by a horse. The hut was small, about two metres by three metres. There was a simple bed at one end, with a barred cage beneath it for a sick or orphaned lamb. Usually, the only other comforts were a stove for warmth and cooking, a wooden table and a chair.

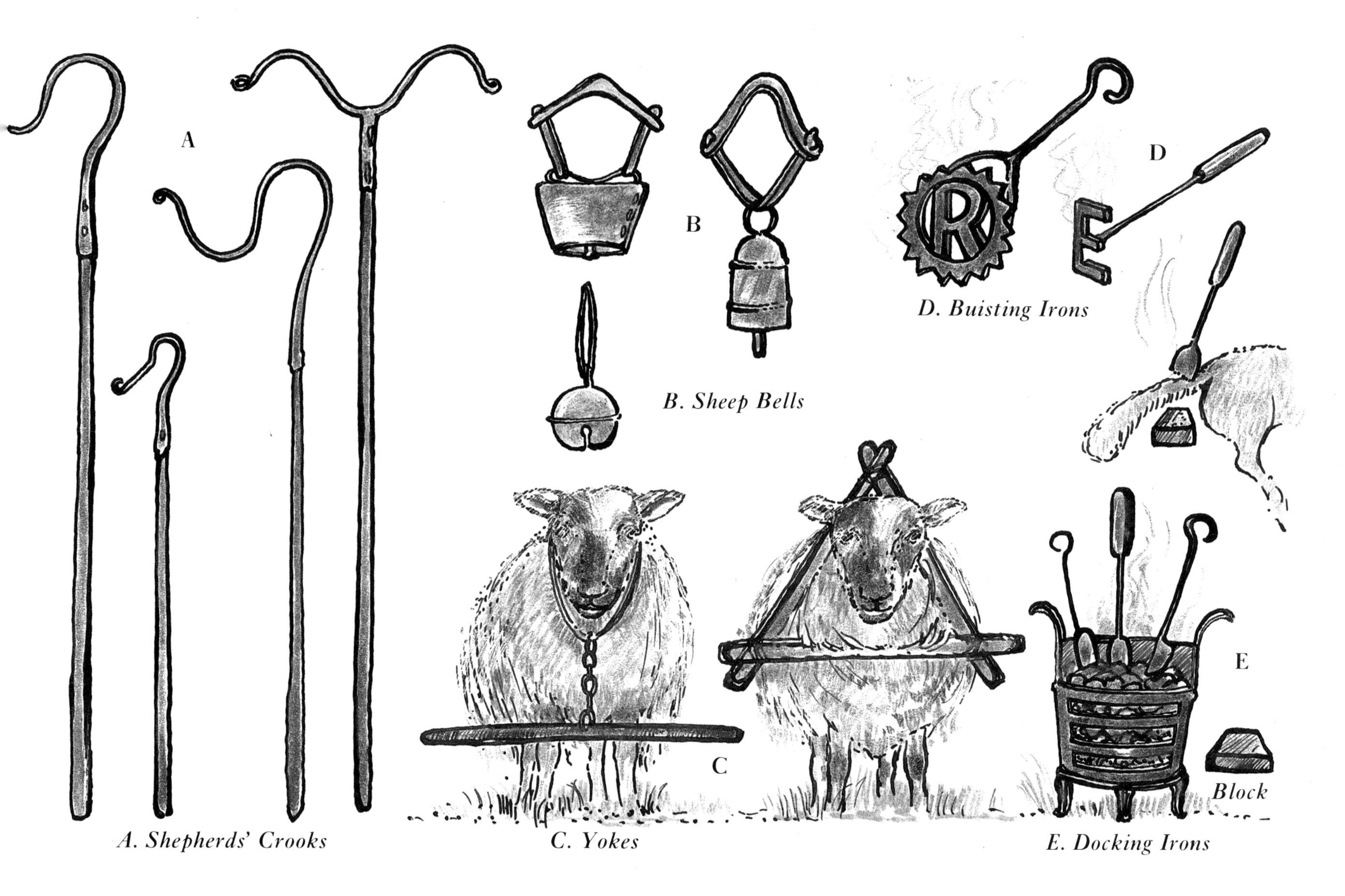

A. Shepherds' Crooks *B. Sheep Bells* *C. Yokes* *D. Buisting Irons* *E. Docking Irons*

A. The iron hoops caught sheep by the leg or neck

B. Sheep bells told the shepherd where the sheep were

C. The yoke prevented sheep escaping through hedges

D. Buisting irons made the owner's mark on the sheep's flank

E. Docking irons were used for docking or searing lambs' tails

SHEEP SHEARING

A skilled man shearing by hand can strip one sheep of its fleece in two minutes and do up to two hundred in a day. He starts at the throat and works with long, sweeping strokes until the fleece is off, then rolls it and ties it in a bundle.

Old hand-shears looked like huge scissors; today's electric shears are more like barbers' clippers.

COPY OF CRUIKSHANK'S CARTOON OF CHILD WORKERS IN TEXTILE MILLS

During the Industrial Revolution conditions in the new factories were terrible. It is known that children as young as five worked up to twelve hours a day.

THE INDUSTRIAL REVOLUTION

Until the late 1700s cloth-making was a cottage industry. Spinning and weaving were done at home on hand machines and workers lived, for the most part, in small rural communities.

The development of huge machines powered by steam brought about a revolution and turned the cottage industry into a factory-based one. Workers moved into fast growing cities, found work in overcrowded factories and lived in terrible conditions, exploited by mill-owners who paid starvation wages and then sold their cloth for good prices at home and abroad.

Having left the villages, the workers were utterly dependent on the mills. The purchase of a large, labour-saving machine by a successful mill-owner could put hundreds out of work. In protest, there were frequent riots when new machinery was smashed. The government supported the mill-owners and punished rioting workers with prison sentences. They also made it illegal for the Guilds to protect their members' rights.

JAMES HARGREAVES' SPINNING JENNY 1764

This spinning machine, a great cost-saver, had a hundred and twenty spindles and could be worked by one operator. Its introduction put many workers out of a job and caused violent protest.

A MODERN SPINNING JENNY

Today's version of the Spinning Jenny covers the factory floor and has thousands of spindles. Even so, it is no more than a giant spinning wheel.

Harris Tweed Symbol

SHETLAND CROFTER WEAVING ON A DOMESTIC LOOM

In spite of the comparative cheapness of machine-woven cloth, there is still a great demand for hand-woven material. This Shetland crofter is working on a hand loom to weave Harris Tweed.

INDEX